PROPHETIC DREAMER
JOURNAL

THIS JOURNAL BELONGS TO:

_____

_____

ISBN 9798986203812

Date: ____/____/____

Scripture Highlight:

_____
_____
_____
_____
_____

Song in My Spirit:

_____
_____
_____
_____
_____

Vision:

_____
_____
_____
_____
_____

Other Forms of Revelation:

_____
_____
_____
_____
_____
_____

Prophetic Word: _____
_____
_____
_____
_____
_____

Gods Still Small Voice: _____
_____
_____
_____
_____
_____

Audible Voice of God: _____
_____
_____
_____
_____
_____

Draw	Action to Take
	_____
	_____
	_____
	_____
	_____
	_____
	_____

Testimony

Date: ___/___/___

Dreams:

Dreams

Date: ___/___/___

Dreams

Date: ___ / ___ / ___

Dreams

Date: ___/___/___

Date: ___/___/___

Scripture Highlight:

_____

_____

_____

_____

_____

_____

Song in My Spirit:

_____

_____

_____

_____

_____

Vision:

_____

_____

_____

_____

_____

Other Forms of Revelation:

_____

_____

_____

_____

_____

Prophetic Word: _____
_____
_____
_____
_____
_____

Gods Still Small Voice: _____
_____
_____
_____
_____
_____

Audible Voice of God: _____
_____
_____
_____
_____
_____

Draw	Action to Take
	_____
	_____
	_____
	_____
	_____
	_____
	_____

Testimony

Date: ___ / ___ / ___

Dreams:

Dreams

Date: ___/___/___

Dreams

Date: ___ / ___ / ___

Dreams

Date: ___/___/___

Date: ___ / ___ / ___

Scripture Highlight:

_____
_____
_____
_____
_____
_____

Song in My Spirit:

_____
_____
_____
_____
_____
_____

Vision:

_____
_____
_____
_____
_____

Other Forms of Revelation:

_____
_____
_____
_____
_____
_____

Prophetic Word:

Gods Still Small Voice:

Audible Voice of God:

Draw	Action to Take

Testimony

Date: ___/___/___

_____

_____

_____

_____

_____

_____

_____

_____

_____

_____

Dreams:

_____

_____

_____

_____

_____

_____

_____

_____

_____

Dreams

Date: ___/___/___

Dreams

Date: ___ / ___ / ___

Dreams

Date: _____ / _____ / _____

Date: ____/____/____

Scripture Highlight:

_____

_____

_____

_____

_____

Song in My Spirit:

_____

_____

_____

_____

_____

Vision:

_____

_____

_____

_____

_____

Other Forms of Revelation:

_____

_____

_____

_____

_____

Prophetic Word:

Gods Still Small Voice:

Audible Voice of God:

Draw	Action to Take

Testimony

Date: ___ / ___ / ___

Dreams:

Dreams

Date: ___/___/___

Dreams

Date: ___ / ___ / ___

Dreams

Date: ___/___/___

Date: _____ / _____ / _____

Scripture Highlight:

_____

_____

_____

_____

_____

Song in My Spirit:

_____

_____

_____

_____

_____

Vision:

_____

_____

_____

_____

_____

Other Forms of Revelation:

_____

_____

_____

_____

_____

_____

Prophetic Word:

Gods Still Small Voice:

Audible Voice of God:

Draw	Action to Take

Testimony

Date: ___ / ___ / ___

Dreams:

Dreams

Date: _____ / _____ / _____

Dreams

Date: ___ / ___ / ___

Dreams

Date: ___ / ___ / ___

Date: ___/___/___

Scripture Highlight:

_____
_____
_____
_____
_____

Song in My Spirit:

_____
_____
_____
_____

Vision:

_____
_____
_____
_____

Other Forms of Revelation:

_____
_____
_____
_____
_____

Prophetic Word:

Gods Still Small Voice:

Audible Voice of God:

Draw	Action to Take

Testimony

Date: _____ / _____ / _____

Dreams:

Date:___/___/___

Dreams

Date: ___/___/___

Dreams

Date: ___/___/___

Date: ___ / ___ / ___

Scripture Highlight:

Song in My Spirit:

Vision:

Other Forms of Revelation:

Prophetic Word:

Gods Still Small Voice:

Audible Voice of God:

Draw	Action to Take

Testimony

Date: ___/___/___

_____
_____
_____
_____
_____
_____
_____
_____
_____
_____
_____

Dreams:
_____
_____
_____
_____
_____
_____
_____
_____
_____
_____

Dreams

Date: ___/___/___

Dreams

Date: ___/___/___

Dreams

Date: ____ / ___ / ____

Date: ___ / ___ / ___

Scripture Highlight:

Song in My Spirit:

Vision:

Other Forms of Revelation:

Prophetic Word:

Gods Still Small Voice:

Audible Voice of God:

Draw	Action to Take

Testimony

Date: ____ / ____ / ____

Dreams:

Dreams

Date: ___/___/___

Dreams

Date: ___ / ___ / ___

Dreams

Date: ___/___/___

Date: ___/___/___

Scripture Highlight:

Song in My Spirit:

Vision:

Other Forms of Revelation:

Prophetic Word:

_____

_____

_____

_____

_____

Gods Still Small Voice:

_____

_____

_____

_____

_____

Audible Voice of God:

_____

_____

_____

_____

_____

Draw	Action to Take
	_____
	_____
	_____
	_____
	_____
	_____
	_____

Testimony

Date: ___ / ___ / ___

Dreams:

Dreams

Date: ___ / ___ / ___

Dreams

Date: ___ /___ /___

Dreams

Date: ___/___/___

Date: ___ / ___ / ___

Scripture Highlight:

Song in My Spirit:

Vision:

Other Forms of Revelation:

Prophetic Word:

Gods Still Small Voice:

Audible Voice of God:

Draw	Action to Take

Testimony

Date: ___ / ___ / ___

Dreams:

Date: ___ / ___ / ___

Dreams

Date: ___/___/___

Dreams

Date: ___/___/___

Date: ___ / ___ / ___

Scripture Highlight: _____

_____

_____

_____

_____

Song in My Spirit: _____

_____

_____

_____

_____

Vision: _____

_____

_____

_____

Other Forms of Revelation: _____

_____

_____

_____

_____

_____

Prophetic Word: _____
_____
_____
_____
_____
_____

Gods Still Small Voice: _____
_____
_____
_____
_____
_____
_____

Audible Voice of God: _____
_____
_____
_____
_____
_____

Draw	Action to Take
	_____
	_____
	_____
	_____
	_____
	_____
	_____

Testimony

Dreams:

Dreams

Date: ___/___/___

Dreams

Date: ___/___/___

Dreams

Date: ___ / ___ / ___

Date: _____ / _____ / _____

Scripture Highlight:

_____

_____

_____

_____

_____

Song in My Spirit:

_____

_____

_____

_____

_____

Vision:

_____

_____

_____

_____

Other Forms of Revelation:

_____

_____

_____

_____

_____

Prophetic Word: _____
_____
_____
_____
_____
_____

Gods Still Small Voice: _____
_____
_____
_____
_____
_____

Audible Voice of God: _____
_____
_____
_____
_____
_____

Draw	Action to Take
	_____
	_____
	_____
	_____
	_____
	_____
	_____

Dreams:

Dreams

Date: ___/___/___

Dreams

Date: ___/___/___

Dreams

Date: ___ / ___ / ___

Date: ___ / ___ / ___

Scripture Highlight:
_____
_____
_____
_____
_____

Song in My Spirit:
_____
_____
_____
_____

Vision:
_____
_____
_____
_____

Other Forms of Revelation:
_____
_____
_____
_____
_____

Prophetic Word: _____
_____
_____
_____
_____
_____

Gods Still Small Voice: _____
_____
_____
_____
_____
_____
_____

Audible Voice of God: _____
_____
_____
_____
_____
_____
_____

Draw	Action to Take
	_____
	_____
	_____
	_____
	_____
	_____
	_____

Testimony

Date: ___ / ___ / ___

Dreams:

Dreams

Date: ___ / ___ / ___

Dreams

Date: ___/___/___

Dreams

Date: ___ / ___ / ___

Date: ___ /___ /___

Scripture Highlight:

Song in My Spirit:

Vision:

Other Forms of Revelation:

Prophetic Word:

Gods Still Small Voice:

Audible Voice of God:

Draw	Action to Take

Testimony

Date: ___/___/___

_____
_____
_____
_____
_____
_____
_____
_____
_____
_____

Dreams:
_____
_____
_____
_____
_____
_____
_____
_____
_____
_____

Date: ___ / ___ / ___

Dreams

Date: ___ / ___ / ___

Dreams

Date: ___ / ___ / ___

Date: ___ / ___ / ___

Scripture Highlight:

_____

_____

_____

_____

_____

Song in My Spirit:

_____

_____

_____

_____

Vision:

_____

_____

_____

_____

Other Forms of Revelation:

_____

_____

_____

_____

_____

Prophetic Word:

_____

_____

_____

_____

_____

Gods Still Small Voice:

_____

_____

_____

_____

_____

_____

Audible Voice of God:

_____

_____

_____

_____

_____

_____

Draw	Action to Take
	_____
	_____
	_____
	_____
	_____
	_____
	_____

Testimony

Date: ___/___/___

Dreams:

Dreams

Date: ___ / ___ / ___

Dreams

Date: ___/___/___

Dreams

Date: ___/___/___

Date: ___/___/___

Scripture Highlight:

Song in My Spirit:

Vision:

Other Forms of Revelation:

Prophetic Word:

_____

_____

_____

_____

_____

Gods Still Small Voice:

_____

_____

_____

_____

_____

Audible Voice of God:

_____

_____

_____

_____

_____

Draw	Action to Take
	_____
	_____
	_____
	_____
	_____
	_____
	_____

Testimony

Date: ___/___/___

Dreams:

Dreams

Date: ___/___/___

Dreams

Date: ___/___/___

Dreams

Date: ___ / ___ / ___

Date: ___ / ___ / ___

Scripture Highlight:

Song in My Spirit:

Vision:

Other Forms of Revelation:

Prophetic Word:

_____
_____
_____
_____
_____
_____

Gods Still Small Voice:

_____
_____
_____
_____
_____

Audible Voice of God:

_____
_____
_____
_____
_____

Draw	Action to Take
	_____
	_____
	_____
	_____
	_____
	_____
	_____

Testimony

Date: ___/___/___

Dreams:

Dreams

Date: ___ / ___ / ___

Date: ___ / ___ / ___

Dreams

Date: ___/___/___

Date: ___/___/___

Scripture Highlight: _____

Song in My Spirit: _____

Vision: _____

Other Forms of Revelation: _____

Prophetic Word:

Gods Still Small Voice:

Audible Voice of God:

Draw	Action to Take

Testimony

Date: ___ / ___ / ___

Dreams:

Dreams

Date: ___/___/___

Dreams

Date: ___/___/___

Dreams

Date: ___/___/___

Date: ___ / ___ / ___

Scripture Highlight: _____

_____

_____

_____

_____

Song in My Spirit: _____

_____

_____

_____

_____

Vision: _____

_____

_____

_____

_____

Other Forms of Revelation: _____

_____

_____

_____

_____

Prophetic Word:

Gods Still Small Voice:

Audible Voice of God:

Draw	Action to Take

Testimony

Date: ___/___/___

Dreams:

Dreams

Date: ___/___/___

Dreams

Date: ___ / ___ / ___

Dreams

Date: ___ / ___ / ___

Date: _____ / _____ / _____

Scripture Highlight:

_____

_____

_____

_____

_____

Song in My Spirit:

_____

_____

_____

_____

_____

Vision:

_____

_____

_____

_____

Other Forms of Revelation:

_____

_____

_____

_____

_____

Prophetic Word:

Gods Still Small Voice:

Audible Voice of God:

Draw	Action to Take

Testimony

Date: ___ / ___ / ___

Dreams:

Dreams

Date: ___/___/___

Dreams

Date: ___/___/___

Dreams

Date: ___/___/___

Date: ___/___/___

Scripture Highlight:

Song in My Spirit:

Vision:

Other Forms of Revelation:

Prophetic Word:

Gods Still Small Voice:

Audible Voice of God:

Draw	Action to Take

Testimony

Date: ___/___/___

Dreams:

Dreams

Date: ___/___/___

Dreams

Date: ___/___/___

Dreams

Date: ___/___/___

Date: ___ / ___ / ___

Scripture Highlight:

Song in My Spirit:

Vision:

Other Forms of Revelation:

Prophetic Word: _____

_____

_____

_____

_____

_____

Gods Still Small Voice: _____

_____

_____

_____

_____

_____

Audible Voice of God: _____

_____

_____

_____

_____

_____

Draw	Action to Take
	_____
	_____
	_____
	_____
	_____
	_____
	_____

Testimony

Date: ___ / ___ / ___

_____

_____

_____

_____

_____

_____

_____

_____

_____

_____

Dreams:

_____

_____

_____

_____

_____

_____

_____

_____

_____

Dreams

Date: ___/___/___

Dreams

Date: ___/___/___

Dreams

Date: ___ / ___ / ___

Date: ___ / ___ / ___

Scripture Highlight:

Song in My Spirit:

Vision:

Other Forms of Revelation:

Prophetic Word:

_____
_____
_____
_____
_____

Gods Still Small Voice:

_____
_____
_____
_____
_____

Audible Voice of God:

_____
_____
_____
_____
_____

Draw	Action to Take
	_____
	_____
	_____
	_____
	_____
	_____

Testimony

Date: ___ / ___ / ___

Dreams:

Dreams

Date: ___ / ___ / ___

Dreams

Date: ___/___/___

Dreams

Date: ___/___/___

Date: _____ / _____ / _____

Scripture Highlight:

_____

_____

_____

_____

_____

Song in My Spirit:

_____

_____

_____

_____

_____

Vision:

_____

_____

_____

_____

_____

Other Forms of Revelation:

_____

_____

_____

_____

_____

_____

Prophetic Word:

Gods Still Small Voice:

Audible Voice of God:

Draw	Action to Take

Testimony

Date: _____ / _____ / _____

Dreams:

Dreams

Date: ___ / ___ / ___

Dreams

Date: ___/___/___

Dreams

Date: ___ / ___ / ___

Date: _____ / _____ / _____

Scripture Highlight:

_____

_____

_____

_____

_____

Song in My Spirit:

_____

_____

_____

_____

_____

Vision:

_____

_____

_____

_____

_____

Other Forms of Revelation:

_____

_____

_____

_____

_____

_____

Prophetic Word:

Gods Still Small Voice:

Audible Voice of God:

Draw	Action to Take

Testimony

Date: ___ / ___ / ___

Dreams:

Dreams

Date: ___ / ___ / ___

Dreams

Date: ___/___/___

Dreams

Date: ___/___/___

Date: _____ / _____ / _____

Scripture Highlight:

_____

_____

_____

_____

_____

Song in My Spirit:

_____

_____

_____

_____

_____

Vision:

_____

_____

_____

_____

_____

Other Forms of Revelation:

_____

_____

_____

_____

_____

Prophetic Word:

Gods Still Small Voice:

Audible Voice of God:

Draw	Action to Take

Testimony

Date: ___ / ___ / ___

Dreams:

Dreams

Date: ___ / ___ / ___

Dreams

Date: ___/___/___

Dreams

Date: ____/____/____

Date: ___/___/___

Scripture Highlight:

_____
_____
_____
_____
_____

Song in My Spirit:

_____
_____
_____
_____
_____

Vision:

_____
_____
_____
_____

Other Forms of Revelation:

_____
_____
_____
_____
_____
_____

Prophetic Word:

Gods Still Small Voice:

Audible Voice of God:

Draw	Action to Take

Testimony

Date: _____ / _____ / _____

_____
_____
_____
_____
_____
_____
_____
_____
_____
_____
_____
_____

Dreams:

_____
_____
_____
_____
_____
_____
_____
_____
_____
_____
_____

Dreams

Date: ___ / ___ / ___

Dreams

Date: ____/____/____

Dreams

Date: ___ / ___ / ___

Date: _____/_____/_____

Scripture Highlight:
_____
_____
_____
_____
_____

Song in My Spirit:
_____
_____
_____
_____
_____

Vision:
_____
_____
_____
_____

Other Forms of Revelation:
_____
_____
_____
_____
_____

Prophetic Word:

Gods Still Small Voice:

Audible Voice of God:

Draw	Action to Take

Testimony

Date: ___ / ___ / ___

Dreams:

Dreams

Date: ___/___/___

Dreams

Date: _____ / _____ / _____

Dreams

Date: ___/___/___

Date: ___/___/___

Scripture Highlight: _____

_____

_____

_____

_____

Song in My Spirit: _____

_____

_____

_____

_____

Vision: _____

_____

_____

_____

Other Forms of Revelation: _____

_____

_____

_____

_____

_____

Prophetic Word:

_____
_____
_____
_____
_____

Gods Still Small Voice:

_____
_____
_____
_____
_____

Audible Voice of God:

_____
_____
_____
_____
_____

Draw	Action to Take
	_____
	_____
	_____
	_____
	_____
	_____
	_____

Testimony

Date: _____/____/_____

Dreams:

Dreams

Date: ___/___/___

Date: ___ / ___ / ___

Dreams

Date: ___ / ___ / ___

Date: ___/___/___

Scripture Highlight:

Song in My Spirit:

Vision:

Other Forms of Revelation:

Prophetic Word:

_____
_____
_____
_____
_____

Gods Still Small Voice:

_____
_____
_____
_____
_____

Audible Voice of God:

_____
_____
_____
_____
_____

Draw	Action to Take
	_____
	_____
	_____
	_____
	_____
	_____
	_____

Testimony

Date: ___/___/___

Dreams:

Dreams

Date: ___ / ___ / ___

Dreams

Date: ___/___/___

Dreams

Date: ___ / ___ / ___

Date: ___ / ___ / ___

Scripture Highlight:

_____
_____
_____
_____
_____

Song in My Spirit:

_____
_____
_____
_____
_____

Vision:

_____
_____
_____
_____

Other Forms of Revelation:

_____
_____
_____
_____
_____
_____

Prophetic Word:

_____

_____

_____

_____

_____

Gods Still Small Voice:

_____

_____

_____

_____

_____

Audible Voice of God:

_____

_____

_____

_____

_____

Draw	Action to Take
	_____
	_____
	_____
	_____
	_____
	_____
	_____

Testimony

Date: _____ / _____ / _____

Dreams:

Dreams

Date: ___ / ___ / ___

Dreams

Date: ___ / ___ / ___

Dreams

Date: ___/___/___

Date: ____/____/____

Scripture Highlight:

Song in My Spirit:

Vision:

Other Forms of Revelation:

Prophetic Word:

Gods Still Small Voice:

Audible Voice of God:

Draw	Action to Take

Testimony

Date: ___ / ___ / ___

_____

_____

_____

_____

_____

_____

_____

_____

_____

_____

_____

Dreams:

_____

_____

_____

_____

_____

_____

_____

_____

_____

Dreams

Date: ___/___/___

Dreams

Date: ___ / ___ / ___

Dreams

Date: ___ / ___ / ___

Date: _____/_____/_____

Scripture Highlight:

_____

_____

_____

_____

_____

Song in My Spirit:

_____

_____

_____

_____

Vision:

_____

_____

_____

_____

Other Forms of Revelation:

_____

_____

_____

_____

_____

_____

Prophetic Word:

Gods Still Small Voice:

Audible Voice of God:

Draw	Action to Take

Testimony

Date: ___/___/___

Dreams:

Dreams

Date: ___ / ___ / ___

Dreams

Date: ___ / ___ / ___

Dreams

Date: ____/____/____

Date: _____ / _____ / _____

Scripture Highlight:

_____
_____
_____
_____
_____

Song in My Spirit:

_____
_____
_____
_____
_____

Vision:

_____
_____
_____
_____
_____

Other Forms of Revelation:

_____
_____
_____
_____
_____

Prophetic Word:

_____
_____
_____
_____
_____

Gods Still Small Voice:

_____
_____
_____
_____
_____

Audible Voice of God:

_____
_____
_____
_____
_____

Draw	Action to Take
	_____
	_____
	_____
	_____
	_____
	_____
	_____

Testimony

Dreams:

Dreams

Date: ___ / ___ / ___

Dreams

Date: ___/___/___

Dreams

Date: ___ / ___ / ___

Date: _____ / _____ / _____

Scripture Highlight:
_____
_____
_____
_____
_____

Song in My Spirit:
_____
_____
_____
_____

Vision:
_____
_____
_____
_____

Other Forms of Revelation:
_____
_____
_____
_____
_____

Prophetic Word:

_____
_____
_____
_____
_____

Gods Still Small Voice:

_____
_____
_____
_____
_____

Audible Voice of God:

_____
_____
_____
_____
_____

Draw	Action to Take
	_____
	_____
	_____
	_____
	_____
	_____
	_____

Testimony

Date: ___ / ___ / ___

Dreams:

Dreams

Date: ___/___/___

Dreams

Date: ___ / ___ / ___

Dreams

Date: ___/___/___

Date: _____ / _____ / _____

Scripture Highlight:

_____

_____

_____

_____

_____

Song in My Spirit:

_____

_____

_____

_____

_____

Vision:

_____

_____

_____

_____

_____

Other Forms of Revelation:

_____

_____

_____

_____

_____

Prophetic Word:

Gods Still Small Voice:

Audible Voice of God:

Draw	Action to Take

Testimony

Date: ___ / ___ / ___

Dreams:

Dreams

Date: ___ / ___ / ___

Dreams

Date: ___ / ___ / ___

Dreams

Date: ___/___/___

Date: ___/___/_____

Scripture Highlight:
_____
_____
_____
_____
_____

Song in My Spirit:
_____
_____
_____
_____

Vision:
_____
_____
_____
_____

Other Forms of Revelation:
_____
_____
_____
_____
_____

Prophetic Word:

Gods Still Small Voice:

Audible Voice of God:

Draw	Action to Take

Testimony

Date: ___/___/___

Dreams:

Dreams

Date: ___/___/___

Dreams

Date: ___/___/___

Dreams

Date: ____/____/____

Date: ___ / ___ / ___

Scripture Highlight: _____

_____

_____

_____

_____

_____

Song in My Spirit: _____

_____

_____

_____

_____

_____

Vision: _____

_____

_____

_____

_____

_____

Other Forms of Revelation: _____

_____

_____

_____

_____

_____

Prophetic Word: _____
_____
_____
_____
_____

Gods Still Small Voice:
_____
_____
_____
_____
_____

Audible Voice of God: _____
_____
_____
_____
_____

Draw	Action to Take
	_____
	_____
	_____
	_____
	_____
	_____

Testimony

Date: ___ / ___ / ___

Dreams:

Dreams

Date: ___ / ___ / ___

Dreams

Date: ___ / ___ / ___

Dreams

Date: ___ / ___ / ___

Made in the USA
Middletown, DE
10 October 2023

40517145R00130